You're Only Old Once!

By Dr. Seuss

RANDOM HOUSE
NEW YORK

Library of Congress Cataloging-in-Publication Data:

Seuss, Dr. You're only old once! I. Title. PS3513.E2Y6 1986 813′.52 85-20495 ISBN: 0-394-55190-7 (trade); 0-394-55395-0 (ltd. ed.)

Manufactured in the United States of America

B9876

With Affection for
and
Afflictions with
the Members of the
Class of 1925

One day you will read
in the *National Geographic*
of a faraway land
with no smelly bad traffic.

In those green-pastured mountains
of Fotta-fa-Zee
everybody feels fine
at a hundred and three
'cause the air that they breathe
is potassium-free
and because they chew nuts
from the Tutt-a-Tutt Tree.
This gives strength to their teeth,
it gives length to their hair,
and they live without doctors,
with nary a care.

And you'll find yourself wishing that *you* were out there
in Fotta-fa-Zee and not here in this chair
in the Golden Years Clinic on Century Square
for Spleen Readjustment and Muffler Repair.

OPTOGLYMICS

DERMOGLYMICS

89A-63B

Just why are you here?
You're not feeling your best...

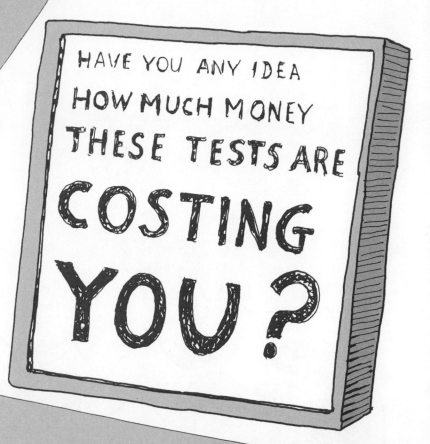

HAVE YOU ANY IDEA
HOW MUCH MONEY
THESE TESTS ARE
COSTING
YOU?

You've come in for
an Eyesight and Solvency Test.

And if you're the type that gets finicky-finick,
at this point you'll try to get out of that clinic.
But they will outwit you as quick as a winick!
The Quiz-Docs will catch you!
They'll start questionnairing!
They'll ask you, point blank, how your parts are all faring.

And your grandfather's parts. And please try to recall
if your grandma hurt most in the spring or the fall.
Did your cousins have dreadful wild nightmares at night?
Did they suffer such ailments as Bus Driver's Blight,
Chimney Sweep's Stupor, or Prune Picker's Plight?
And describe the main cause of your uncle's collapse.
Too much alphabet soup? Or martinis, perhaps?

And the next thing you know,
when you've finished *that* test,
is somehow you've lost
both your necktie and vest
and an Ogler is ogling
your stomach and chest.

Your escape plans have melted!
You haven't a chance,
for the next thing you know,
both your socks and your pants
and your drawers and your shoes
have been lost for the day.
The Oglers have blossomed
like roses in May!
And silently, grimly, they ogle away.

Signs in the hallway: 3X – 3K, 61-82, NOORONETICS

What those Oglers have learned
they're not ready to tell.
Clinicians don't spout
their opinions pell-mell.
So you're back
with the vestibule fish for a spell.
Norval won't bring you
much comfort, you know.
But he's quite sympathetic
as Clinic Fish go.

61-82

NLDCA

NOORONETICS

There you'll sit several hours, growing tenser each second,
fearing your fate will be worse than you reckoned,
till finally Miss Becker, your beckoner, beckons...

...to a booth where the World-Renowned Ear Man, Von Crandall,
has perfected a test known as Bellows and Candle.
If the wind from the bellows can't blow out the flame,
you failed! And you're going to be sorry you came.

You'll be told that your hearing's so murky and muddy,
your case calls for special intensified study.
They'll test you with noises from far and from near
and you'll get a black mark for the ones you can't hear.
Then they'll say, "My dear fellow, you're deafer than most.
But there's hope, since you're not quite as deaf as a post.
We'll study your symptoms. We'll give you a call.
In the meantime, go back and sit down in the hall."

So you'll find yourself talking to Norval once more.
And Norval will think you're a bit of a bore
because Norval has heard the same stories before.

To this fish you'll become
a plain pain in the neck
while you wait, once again,
for Miss Becker to beck.

But Miss Becker *won't* come.
With great swish and great swank
a wheelchair will come!
You've gained status and rank!
And Whelden the Wheeler will say with great pride:
"You have qualified, sir.
You are now certified
as a VIP Case.
You're entitled to ride!
Through thin and through thick
I'll be at your back side."

Dear Whelden will show you great sights as you go:
Right now you are riding down Stethoscope Row.
And I know that, like all our top patients, you're hoping
to get yourself stethed with some fine first-class scoping.
So I'm sure you'll be simply delighted to hear
that in the Internal Organs Olympics last year
Doctors Schmidt, Smoot, Sinatra, Sylvester, and Fonz
won fifteen gold medals,
nine silver,
six bronze!
For the moment, however, we'll by-pass this bunch.
There is plenty of time to see *them* after lunch.

You must see Dr. Pollen, our Allergy Whiz,
who knows every sniffle and itch that there is.
Dr. Pollen will find, as he works on your case,
if the face powder's wrong on your stepsister's face.
He will check your reactions to thumbtacks and glue,
catcher's mitts, leaf mold, and cardigans, too,
nasturtiums and marble cake, white and blue chalks,
anthracite coal and the feathers of hawks.
Also corn on the cob. Also buffalo grease
and how you react when you're stared at by geese.
He'll take copious notes. Then I'll hazard a guess
that he'll send you downstairs to see Dr. Van Ness.

Van Ness has enjoyed a high rate of success
in his pioneer work in the Study of Stress.
So, you can be sure, he will stress you a trifle,
then he'll send you around to see Dr. Von Eiffel.

Dietician Von Eiffel controls the *Wuff-Whiffer,*
our Diet-Devising Computerized Sniffer,
on which you just simply lie down in repose
and sniff at good food as it goes past your nose.
From caviar soufflé to caribou roast,
from pemmican patties to terrapin toast,
he'll find out by Sniff-Scan the foods you like most.

And when that guy finds out
what you like,
you can bet it
won't be on your diet.
From here on, forget it!

Then, into the New Wing! We'll see Dr. Spreckles,
who does the *Three F's*—Footsies, Fungus, and Freckles.
And nextly we'll drop in on young Dr. Ginns,
our *A and S Man* who does Antrums and Shins,
and of course *he'll* refer us to Doctors McGrew,
McGuire and McPherson and Blinn and Ballew
and Timpkins and Tompkins and Diller and Drew,
Fitzsimmons, Fitzgerald, and Fitzpatrick, too,
all of whom will prescribe a prescription for you.

For your Pill Drill you'll go to Room Six Sixty-three,
where a voice will instruct you, *"Repeat after me...*
This small white pill is what I munch
at breakfast and right after lunch.
I take the pill that's kelly green
before each meal and in between.
These loganberry-colored pills
I take for early morning chills.
I take the pill with zebra stripes
to cure my early evening gripes.
These orange-tinted ones, of course,
I take to cure my charley horse.

PILL

"I take three blues at half past eight
to slow my exhalation rate.
On alternate nights at nine p.m.
I swallow pinkies. Four of them.
The reds, which make my eyebrows strong,
I eat like popcorn all day long.
The speckled browns are what I keep
beside my bed to help me sleep.
This long flat one is what I take
if I should die before I wake."

When at last we are sure
you've been properly pilled,
then a few paper forms
must be properly filled
so that you and your heirs
may be properly billed.

FORE

AFT

Whereupon...
if you're smart,
there's a very good chance
that you'll meet soon again
with your socks, coat, and pants.

And you'll know,
once your necktie's
back under your chin
and Norval has waved you
Godspeed with his fin,
you're in pretty good shape
for the shape you are in!